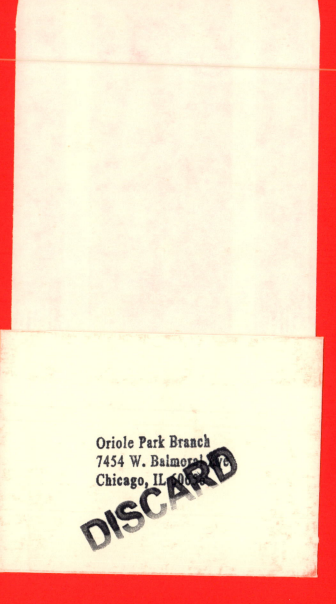

EXPERIMENT WITH
MOVEMENT

Written by Bryan Murphy

Science Consultant: Dr. Christine Sutton
Nuclear Physics Department, University of Oxford

Education Consultant: Ruth Bessant

TWO CAN™

PRINCETON ▪ LONDON

www.two-canpublishing.com

Published in the United States and Canada by
Two-Can Publishing LLC
234 Nassau Street
Princeton, NJ 08542

For information on Two-Can books and multimedia,
call 1-609-921-6700, fax 1-609-921-3349, or visit our Web site at
http://www.two-canpublishing.com

Author: Bryan Murphy
Illustrator: Sally Kindberg
Designer: Linda Blakemore
Science Consultant: Dr. Christine Sutton
Education Consultant: Ruth Bessant

hc ISBN 1-58728-248-8
sc ISBN 1-58728-116-3

hc 1 2 3 4 5 6 7 8 9 10 02 01
sc 1 2 3 4 5 6 7 8 9 10 02 01

Printed in Hong Kong

CONTENTS

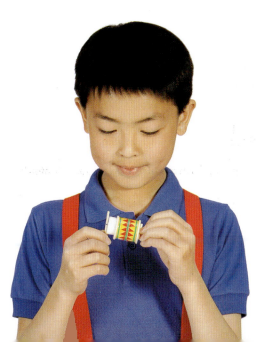

WHAT IS MOVEMENT?

Sit very still and look around you. What do you notice? Is anything moving?

Some things move very quickly, like rockets and airplanes. Flying birds and cars move much more slowly than rockets do, but they are quite fast when compared to real slow-pokes, like snails.

Here are some pictures of things that move. Rank them in order, from fastest to slowest.

WHERE DO FORCES COME FROM?

Everything that moves does so because of something called a **force**. Force is power that makes something happen. Imagine what the world would be like if everything stayed exactly where it was.

Forces can sometimes hurt you, so be very careful when you do any of the experiments in this book.

Here is a way of making an indoor rocket. You will need a long piece of thin string, a short straw (about four inches or 10 centimeters long), and a sausage-shaped balloon.

● Thread the string through the straw and tie the ends to two chairs placed across from each other.
● Blow up the balloon and hold the opening closed so air does not escape.
● Ask someone to carefully tape the bottom side of the balloon (along the long edge) to the straw, while you continue to hold the balloon shut. Next, move the balloon back.
● Then, quickly let go of the balloon.

What happened? As the air in the balloon escaped, it pushed the rocket forward, along the string. Try using a different-shaped balloon or different types and thicknesses of string.

This is an experiment to make a windup toy. You will need an empty thread spool, a rubber—or **elastic**—band, half of a toothpick, some tape, a candle, and a whole toothpick.

● Ask an adult to cut a slice from the end of the candle.

● Smooth off the top and bottom of the candle slice by rubbing it against newspaper pages.

● Ask an adult to make a hole through the middle of the candle slice.

● Thread the rubber band through the holes in the spool and candle slice. With the half toothpick, hold the rubber band in place at the opposite end of the spool from the candle.

● Secure the half toothpick to the spool with a small piece of tape.

● Insert the whole toothpick through the rubber band loop so it rubs against the wax.

● Wind the rubber band tight against the candle slice, using the toothpick to turn it.

● Put the toy on a table, let go, and watch. The **energy** stored in the wound-up rubber band pushes the toy forward.

FORCES AT WORK

If a force pushes or pulls something, different things can happen. You can create forces to move and shape things yourself. When you make something out of modeling clay, you are using different forces. You can push the clay between your fingers to flatten it. You can also squeeze and pull the clay apart to make it into long sausages. How many different shapes can you make?

You can make your own pinwheel from heavy paper, two beads, a long pin, and a pencil with an eraser.

▶ Trace this shape onto the paper. Cut along the solid lines. Next, bend each tip, called a vane, into the center without making a sharp, folded edge. Place a bead on the pin, and stick the pin through the center of the pinwheel. Put the other bead on the pin, and pin the pinwheel onto the pencil eraser.

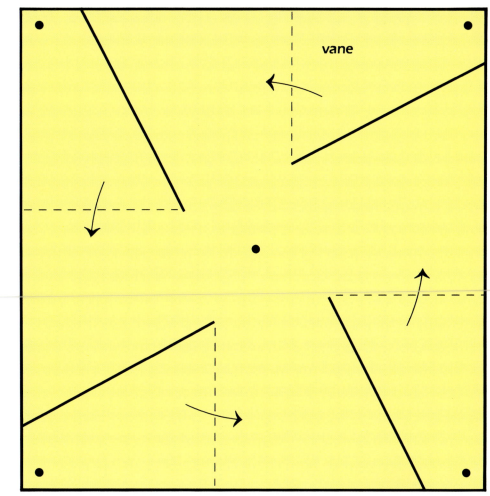

vane

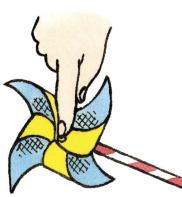

What happens if you move your pinwheel through the air? The air exerts a force to make the pinwheel spin. See if you can make the pinwheel move even better by changing the shape of the vanes or making them bigger.

HOW DO WE MOVE?

It is nearly impossible for us to sit entirely still. We are always moving. We breathe, walk, run, jump, climb, and swim. How many other ways of moving can you think of?

How do we move? This girl has a strong **skeleton**, which gives her the right shape. Her bones are joined in many ways so that she can move. She has some **joints** that bend, like elbows and knees, and others that rotate, like wrists and ankles. **Muscles** are attached to her bones to make them move.

There are more than 600 muscles in your body that are pulling on your bones to make them work.

Try making a model arm to see how the muscles work. You will need some thick cardboard, a round-head fastener (which is a large pin with two legs that bend to form a clip), and two small rubber bands.

Cut these shapes out of thick cardboard by first tracing the patterns on a thin sheet of paper. Then cut them out, and draw around them onto the cardboard. Poke holes where the circles are marked. Make an elbow joint by inserting the fastener through the two holes. Now you have the joint. Rubber bands will act as muscles to provide the forces.

shoulder

A
(biceps)

B
(triceps)

holes for round-head fastener

A

O

lower arm

O

B

The muscle in the front of the upper arm is called the **biceps** and the muscle in the back of the upper arm is the **triceps**. Hook the first rubber band onto the points marked A and the second rubber band onto the points marked B. Now see what happens to the "muscles" when you make the joint swing up and down. Compare the model to your own arm by lifting something heavy. You can feel your biceps pulling your lower arm upward.

FORCES IN THE PLAYGROUND

Forces can be great fun. Visit a playground to see what you can do with different types of force. Remember always to be careful when you are playing on the equipment. You can be moving very fast, and the ground is likely to be very hard.

▶ Try a swing. By moving your legs back and forth, you can make the swing go higher and higher. There is a force called **gravity** that pulls you downward again. Another force, **inertia**, keeps you from stopping at the bottom, so you continue moving backward and forward.

▼ Next, ride on the merry-go-round. As it turns, you can feel **centrifugal force** pulling your body outward.

▶ Now try the slide. Gravity does all the work for you, pulling you downward. Look at the surface of the slide. To work best, it has to be very smooth so that you can slip down it easily. What do you think would happen if the slide had a rough surface?

Set a tray at an angle against several
building blocks or books to make a ramp.
Choose a selection of heavy and light
objects and try sliding them from the top
of the tray. Do some things slide down
more quickly than others? Do the objects
slide faster if you wet the tray? Take away
some of the blocks or books to change
the slope of the tray. What difference does
this make in how things will slide?

SLOWING DOWN

Whenever things touch, there is always a force called **friction** that stops them from slipping. If it was not for friction, the world would be a very strange place. Everything would keep sliding. Imagine what would happen if we tried to move. Our shoes would not grip the floor and we would fall over.

In some places friction is helpful, and in others we try to get rid of it so that things move more easily. You can find many examples of friction on a bicycle.

Turn a bicycle upside-down and rotate the pedals until the back wheel is spinning really fast. How long does it take for the wheel to slow down and stop? The **ball bearings** inside the center of the wheel make a lot of noise because they rub together. Friction between the ball bearings slows the wheel down. If you put some grease on the ball bearings, there will be less friction, and the wheel will turn even more easily.

▼ Look at the chain. If you put household oil on it, the chain will move easily over the **cogs** to spin the wheel around.

▲ Friction can be very useful as well. As you pedal fast or go around a sharp curve, the tires have to be rough enough to grip the surface without slipping.

There is one place where friction is very important. If you want to stop quickly, your bicycle brakes have to provide a lot of force. You create a lot of friction between the rubber brake blocks and the metal wheel rims when you apply the brakes.

There are many other examples of friction on a bicycle. See if you can find out where they are. You must take care of your bike and keep it in good condition, because you never know when you are going to need friction.

MOVING FAST

There is also friction when things move in air or water. Friction caused by air is called **drag**. Racing cars are specially shaped to reduce drag. A smooth, **streamlined** design cuts down the amount of friction and helps the cars move very fast.

This boat has been designed to cut through the water very quickly. It too has a curved, streamlined hull that is very smooth, so there is little friction. The water glides easily around the surface of the hull so that the boat can skim fast over the waves.

Have you ever rubbed your hands together to keep warm on a cold day? As you move your hands, friction makes heat. In the same way, when a space rocket returns to Earth, friction between the air and the rocket makes the rocket's surface get very hot. Space rockets are covered with special heat-proof tiles to keep the astronauts cool.

BIG MACHINES

Ask an adult to take you to visit a building site. You will see lots of huge machines there. Imagine how much more work people would have to do if they did not have machines. How long would they have to work to build houses, schools, stores, and offices?

Big machines use powerful forces. On these pages, you can see a machine that mixes cement and another that scoops up earth like a giant shovel.

Did you know that paste is a type of cement? You can make your own paste to stick your paper models together.

Measure out one mug of flour and three mugs of water.

In a saucepan, mix a little of the water with the flour to make a smooth paste.

Add the rest of the water and ask an adult to heat the mixture until it boils, stirring it all the time. With the heat turned down, the mixture should simmer until the paste thickens.

Like cement, paste holds things together and resists forces that might pull those things apart.

GEARS ARE GREAT

Many machines use **gears** to run properly. Big machines like cars and small machines like clocks have gears. Many gears are made of metal so that they last a long time. Oil keeps them cool and reduces friction to help them turn easily.

▶ Look at this enlarged picture of the inside of a windup wristwatch. The gears are actually very small, but they make the hands of the watch move at exactly the right speed. The ticking sound that you can hear from the watch is the sound of the gears moving. Digital watches work differently and do not use gears. What kind of watch do you have?

A gearwheel has teeth around its edges that mesh, or lock, into those of another gearwheel. When one gearwheel moves around, it forces its neighboring gearwheel to turn as well.

Gears move power from one part of a machine to another. They can also be used to make parts turn faster or slower.

This **windmill** uses gears to turn its sails. If you have a building kit with gear-wheels, try building a model using one, two, three, or more gearwheels. Does it become harder or easier to turn the parts of your model with fewer or more gears? Can you think of any machines around your home that use gears?

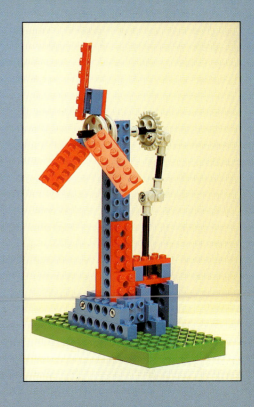

PULLEYS AND ROLLERS

One way of moving things is to drag them over a surface. This can be difficult, because there is friction between the object and the surface. Putting oil on a smooth floor would lessen the friction, but you would make a big mess that might cause people to fall over.

▼ You can make something easier to move by putting it on **rollers**, such as rolling pins or pencils. Instead of dragging along the surface, the object will roll along without much friction.

▲ A **pulley** is a wheel with a rope around it. Pulleys are used at many building sites to lift heavy loads.

◀ You can increase your ability to move heavy objects by using something like a pulley. Here is a trick that makes you stronger than two friends. You need about six yards (or six meters) of rope, two broomsticks, and two strong friends. Give each of them a broomstick and ask them to stand facing each other, holding their broomsticks in front of them. Now tie the end of the rope to one broomstick and loop it around both broomsticks several times. If you pull on the rope, you should be able to pull your friends together. No matter how hard they pull apart, you will always be stronger.

▼ Obviously, round rollers work very well, but did you know that rollers do not have to be circular to roll evenly? These shapes work just as well as round rollers.

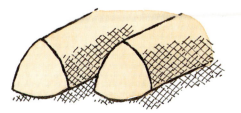

LEVERS

A **lever** can turn a small force into a big one. There are many examples of levers around most houses.

▶ A wrench pushes a metal nut around with a very big force.

◀ You would have a very difficult time cracking a walnut with your hands, but a nutcracker gives you the force to do it.

▶ Tell your friends that you are strong enough to lift them with one hand. Can you think of a way to do it with a lever? Put a long, thick plank of wood on the ground. Then place a brick under the plank a short distance from one end. If your friends stand on the end closest to the brick, you can lift them easily by pushing down on the other end of the plank. What would happen if they stood on the end farthest from the brick? Move the brick closer to the middle of the plank. Is it harder or easier to lift your friends?

FAST FOOD

Food is very important for our bodies. It does much more than just taste nice and stop us from feeling hungry. Food gives us energy to live, run, and jump—just as cars and trains need fuel to move. If we do not eat enough of the right foods, we feel tired and grumpy.

There are different types of food—carbohydrates, proteins, and fats. We need to eat some from each type to keep healthy.

Rice, bread, pasta, and potatoes are all foods that give us energy. They are called carbohydrates. Before a long race, marathon runners usually eat a pasta meal. They eat platefuls of spaghetti to give them energy to run.

Athletes eat a lot of food containing proteins to make their bodies strong. Proteins are found in cheese, grains, meat, and beans.

People also need to eat some fats from foods like milk, margarine, and ice cream.

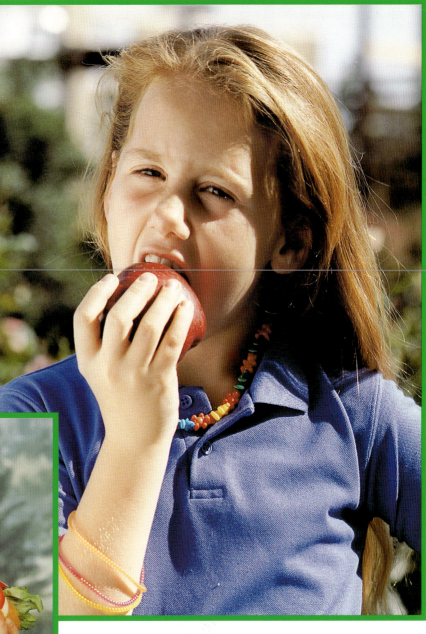

If you want to stay healthy, try not to eat too many foods like cake, candy, or potato chips. Your body does not need these to stay alive. Fish, fruits, and vegetables are all good for you. Some people do not eat meat. They stay healthy by eating other food that contains proteins. What did you eat today?

Children should drink three large glasses of milk every day to keep teeth and bones healthy.

GRAVITY

Gravity is the force that pulls everything down toward the Earth. Imagine what life would be like without it. Walking would be impossible because your feet would not touch the floor. Things would not stay where you left them because they would float around the room like an astronaut in outer space.

Sometimes gravity can be a nuisance. When things fall, they might break when they hit the ground, like an egg hitting the kitchen floor.

Some things bounce. You can make a really bouncy ball in your own kitchen. You need some white school glue and some boric acid powder, which you can buy at a drugstore. Boric acid powder is a chemical that you should use only when an adult is watching.

▶ Put one teaspoon of boric acid powder in a teacup and dissolve it in two teaspoons of warm water. Then add one tablespoon of glue and mix it very quickly into the boric acid solution. Shape the mixture in your hands. What happens? The runny glue becomes like a bouncy rubber ball.

▼ Add food colors to make your ball prettier. Try putting more or less boric acid powder in the mixture and see if it makes the ball even bouncier.

Be careful with your ball, though—it could stain the furniture.

GLOSSARY

ball bearings: metal balls used to reduce friction and help pieces slide over one another

biceps: the large muscle in the front of the upper arm which raises the forearm

centrifugal force: the force that pulls a spinning object outward

cogs: rows of teeth on a wheel

drag: friction caused by air

elastic: able to stretch and bounce back

energy: the power to do work

force: the power that causes an object to move, stop, or change directions

friction: the force that slows down a moving object that is in contact with a surface

gears: two or more toothed wheels that fit together and cause each other to move

gravity: the force that pulls things toward the ground

inertia: the force in an object that helps it to resist stopping if it is already moving or to resist moving if it is stopped

joint: the place where two bones join

lever: a bar (set on a fixed point) that can be moved to help lift heavy objects or move other objects

muscles: tissues in the body that pull on bones and help you to move

pulley: a wheel with a rope around it, used for lifting or moving heavy objects

rollers: cylinders that can be used to move a heavy object over a surface. They turn smoothly and reduce the friction between the object and the surface.

skeleton: the bones that give a body its shape

streamlined: shaped to travel smoothly through liquid or air

triceps: the large muscle in the back of the upper arm that pulls the forearm down

windmill: a shaft with large blades that uses wind energy to create electricity or operate machinery

31

INDEX

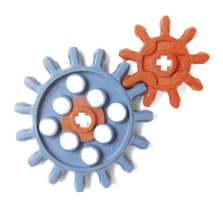